HAVE THE CAREER YOU WANT – PLAY IT AS YOU PLAN IT

Daniel O. Cohen Sr.

RayRay Press, Ewa Beach, HI
ISBN: 978-0-578-58867-4
Title: *Have the Career You Want* / Daniel O. Cohen Sr.
Formats available:
Digital edition
Print edition

This book is dedicated to my Grandson Khalil. May you experience success in life, and the jobs you select to build your career, bring you development, happiness, and fulfillment.

This book is also dedicated to my Father Joseph Cohen Sr. Thank you for being a positive role model and showing me how to find my passion, develop my skills, and letting me be me.

Table of Contents

Forward
The Opening Move

I failed the second grade. I remember being told by my older siblings how difficult the second grade was compared to the first grade. Believe me, I had a mental block trying to figure out each subject. Being a second grader, I didn't know about things like the Self-Fulfilling Prophecy, or positive thinking. I just wanted to play! If someone asked me, what do you want to be when you grow up? I'd respond that I wanted to be a police officer or fireman. You know, the old "go-to" career choice of most kids.

During this time, our family lived in Sierra Vista, Arizona. It was in the early 1960s and my father was in the army and he was doing the first of two tours of duty in Vietnam. Mom was holding down the home front, and my big sister was in charge of me and my siblings while mom was at work. Growing up in Arizona was fun. I actually remember learning how to walk as my mom and big sister guided me between them.

The elementary school I attended was not diverse at all, well it was the sixties. There were three people of color in the school, my older sister Linda, my older brother Joseph Jr., and me. We stood out as most African Americans lived in the south and north back then, nevertheless Arizona. Most people in the sixties, in Arizona, only saw black people on TV. So, I got use to other kids feeling my skin and rubbing my hair because I looked different. Being a minority at school, university and the workplace became a theme in my life.. I was often treated differently because of the color of my skin.

Spending time by myself was alright with me. Entertainment for me was watching the red ants fight the black ants. Talk about an all-out war! I enjoyed climbing trees, hiking, and throwing rocks. Before we plugged into the internet, we made up our own games. Growing up, we had to be creative and it was fun! Trying to derail a train by putting a penny on the track to out running dogs while on the way to the country store to buy penny candy. Dividing into to two teams and going deep into the woods to play war and capture opponent's flag. We had to work as a team when we played. Well, I guess kids do the same today, they just do it virtually. But there is nothing like being able to experience the same game in real life. Life lessons happen in real life too.

You know, I didn't learn what an introvert was until I was in my thirties, but I am definitely one of those quiet people. I was that quiet kid, a young adult with the mindset to mind his own business. People drain my ENERGY. Funny, now people are my business and understanding human dynamics within the workplace is at the cornerstone of what I do. Self-awareness is at the center of improvement. Without self-awareness, no level of coaching will work. You cannot guide someone who does not know where their opportunities lie for improvement. The most successful people know where their gaps are in development and acknowledge there is room for improvement.

Now back to the report card. Incapable of learning. I believe that was the note on my report card at the end of the second grade school year. But what I did not know at that time was, "Learner" is one of my top five Strength Finder strengths. Looking back, I chalked up my second-grade failure to the old Self-Fulfilling Prophecy. I knew the second grade was hard, so it became hard. But what I realized later in life was, that I loved to learn, and I became a student of learning. I had leveraged a strength that I did not know I had. Being curious and wanting to know why things were the way they were. What if? Why not? How come?

I was that kid that looked through every page of the encyclopedia starting with category A going all the way through category Z. Back then, information was sold to you by a traveling encyclopedia salesperson. My dad would sit with the salesperson in our living room and look at encyclopedias, and determine the quality amongst other features. Once we had our new set, I would thumb through them. Hey, there is a country called Peru! Peru, how many people, what do they look like? How did the country come to be? A lot of things to learn about the world, but you had to wait for the next year's version of the encyclopedia for the update. Yeah, seems so funny now when you can get instant information from the internet. Access to vast amounts of information! Assuming it is true. Nevertheless, information is at your fingertips. But what boggles my mind today is most people can't tell you a country or its capital if you pointed it out on a globe. Or name all the USA states and capitals. That's another story.

By the time I graduated from high school at the age of sixteen, fear of failure was my motivator. I remember lying in bed on graduation day after the ceremony, scared to death of the thought of failing in life. I mean an overwhelming fear of failure. What I did not realize at that time was fear of failure became a motivator for me. In addition, I did not know that "Learner" was one of my top five strengths. The love for learning helped me develop my knowledge, skills, and abilities once I entered the world of work. To learn was natural to me, and to learn means to develop.

After high school, it was game time and off to college to study Mechanical Engineering Technology at South Carolina State University. And then things changed for me. I left the university after my sophomore year because I could not afford the expense, so it was time to go to work. I landed a job as a Management Trainee for a large textile company. Key word here is job. The textile industry was going through turbulent times in the USA, and the company I worked for had not kept up with technological changes, leadership practices, and just sound fundamental management. The company relied on them being "*the largest textile company in the world.*" And that was true, but you can't remain number one when the organization fails to transform. So, I learned very quickly that never join a company that does not invest in their people, processes, and practices. I quit after two years and learned how not to manage from the autocratic managers I had to work for. You know the leave your brain at the door and I will tell you what to do type managers.

Like many people, we start our career in one field, then wind up doing something totally different. When I started working I did not think about a career, I just wanted a job that paid well. I put no thought into my personal development, or if the job I was doing was the job I should have been doing. I just floated from one job to a better paying job. Nevertheless, I made one lucky move back then that landed me in a job for the South Carolina State Board for Technical & Comprehensive Education. Yeah, that's a mouthful. Basically, it was the Technical Community College system and I was a Training Specialist responsible for designing, developing and evaluating training programs. My main external customer was new and expanding industries that had moved into the state. Luckily, in that job, I was surrounded by over two dozen Human Resource executives that were working on their second careers as state employees. What I learned from these experienced leaders was priceless.

What I did not realize back then was the power of being coached or having a sponsor. I worked hard, paid attention to others and my work, and tried my best to stay out of the Human Resources office. After all, what I knew at the time was if you worked hard, you would get ahead. Wrong! Working hard is only part of the equation and obviously important though. I can't recall in my career where people advanced if they did not put in effective effort. On the other hand, the development I received in that job as a Training Specialist was the foundation that started me down the path of having a career in Human Resources.

What I learned in that job was I absolutely love doing presentations. A friend once told me that I am a different person when I am on stage presenting. That friend also told me that my voice changes when I talk about numbers. Yes I love numbers and everything that involves numbers. You see, when you do something you love, time flies and there is not enough time in the day.

Fast forward to my current role and find myself sitting here on assignment for the second time in beautiful Maui Hawaii, working for one of the best companies in the world. A lot has transpired since the opening move of my career, and as I enter the latter stage, I want to share what I have seen over three decades in the corporate workplace. In particular, how does one manage their career to achieve their dreams, and happiness. We spend most of our lifetime at work yet many of us leave our careers and time spent at work to chance only to have unfulfilled dreams when we retire.

I remember going into every interview with this thought, "life comes down to a few moments, and this is one of those moments." What I did not realize is how true that statement was and is, as it's timeless. We have few precious choices when it comes to selecting the right opportunities for development, selecting the right coaches and being selected by the right sponsors. Make wise choices as your career will depend on it, and will have an immense impact on your career outcome and satisfaction.

At the end of our work life cycle, career satisfaction does not come from what job you do, it will come from who you get to be while doing that job. And who you get to be is the genuine you. The question is, are you able to be the real you in your current job? Career? Or are you faking it until you make it?

Chapter One
Interest vs. Passion

I learned how to cook from my dad when I was eleven years old. My dad Joseph Cohen Sr. is a chef and my grandmother Ruth Cohen was a great cook too. Cooking is a talent that runs in the family. If you are going to cook a meal in the Cohen household, you better bring you're "A" game. Passion for cooking runs deep within the family and you could not escape cooking meals either. Our family consisted of three girls and three boys, and each of us had a day we were responsible for cooking. My day to cook was Thursday. Because of their courage and candor, siblings can be very good food critics. I cooked chili every Thursday until I got it right, and this drove my siblings mad!

Early in my career I worked for a state government department in South Carolina. During this time, I met a friend named Armando. Armando was from the Philippines and he liked to cook too. Living in a small town in South Carolina with little to do, Armando and I decided to share recipes. I would cook southern soul food, and Armando would cook Philippines food. First time I ever tasted a cooked shrimp with the head still on was in a dish cooked by my Filipino friend Armando.

One day Armando asked me if I knew how to play chess. I replied, "no but teach me." Armando began to teach me the basics of chess. After meals we would play several games of chess and Armando would beat me really bad, and then yell, and I mean yell while laughing, "Go read a book!" This treatment went on for six months, I would lose, and Armando would take pleasure beating me in chess. Armando was a civil engineer and designed bridges for a living. Well, he knew strategy and was a very disciplined person. I got close to beating Armando a few times, but I never did. Time passed and as with many early in career people, transfers happen and we parted ways for our next jobs.

I moved to Columbia, South Carolina, and realized I needed a new chess partner, but did not know many people in the new city I was living in. One Saturday I came across this nice computer chess board at Radio Shack and I bought it. It had sixty-four levels ranging from novice up to grand master! I began to play daily and once I had beaten a level seven times in a row, I would advance to the next level. The game of chess had my interest! I kept two things in my Nineteen Eighty Triumph Spitfire, my saxophone, and my chess board. Every time I would meet a fellow chess player, I would challenge them to a match.

Several years had passed since my chess beatings from Armando, and I had gotten better. As a matter of fact, I was cocky about getting better too. You see, I would keep up with my wins and losses each year. This particular year my record was eighty-six wins and three losses. I was beating people all across the state. I went as far as telling people that I was a good chess player. After all, my record showed the objective evidence! Play me, and you will lose! Well, there is a high probability that you will lose.

Then it happened! It started like any challenge. One Saturday afternoon a stranger said, "you wanna play chess?" and I replied, "absolutely!" We set the chess board up and it was my move first. I played aggressive and got myself into trouble early in the match. I realized quickly the stranger was good. I lost the match during the middle game. I did not even make it to the third stage which is the end game. You see in chess, there are three stages in a match, an opening, middlegame, and endgame. I had never been beaten that bad in a match! My pride kicked in, and I said to the stranger, "let's go again.". Nevertheless, the second game was more of the same but faster. Then the third, fourth, fifth, sixth and FINALLY the seventh loss! Who is this chess super hero! Then the stranger disclosed he was ranked third in the state of South Carolina. What! Oh, so I just played a professional. chess player. But there was a significant difference between us. I had interest in playing chess. Chess was a hobby for me as I did not practice every day or compete in tournaments. I didn't have a chess coach or a sponsor. Chess was a hobby that I had interest in playing. On the other hand, the stranger loved chess so much that he dedicated his passion and talent to the game of chess. He had picked chess as a career and devoted to improving his talent, which comprised of his knowledge, skills, and ability for the game. After all he competed with the best.

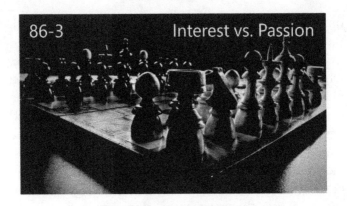

(Interest) in·ter·est

NOUN
1. the state of wanting to know or learn about something or someone

(Passion) pas·sion

NOUN
1. strong and barely controllable emotion.

My interest in learning chess took my ability to a different level. But I didn't have barely controllable emotion about the game. Have you ever been to a restaurant and the waiter or waitress just does not seem to care about you, your order, or taking care of you during your meal. Then you have those moments when you get lucky and come across a gem. A waitress or waiter that seems to care, and flawlessly makes your dinner experience a joy. You can't teach passion, you either have it or you don't. You can teach a person with interest in a subject or job, but you will get a certain level of performance. In sports, the best players get put into the game, while the second and third strings are on the bench waiting for

4

an opportunity. The backups made the team, but they are not to go to people. What separates the different strings? They all have worked hard to get to their levels of performance. But what really separates them? I believe people with passion will always outperform people that have an interest.

In my office, on a table sits the very same chess board I purchased at Radio Shack. Why? To remind me of the difference between interest and passion. For many years, a coaching session would start with someone telling me, I'm interested in HR, or I'm interested in being a manager, leader, CEO, trainer, engineer and the list goes on and on. Now there is nothing wrong with following an interest. Just don't make your interest your career. There may be times in your career that you have to take a job you are interested in to close a development gap. Each job we earn will have either a positive or negative consequence in our career. The choices you make will determine if you have a series of jobs along the way, or a fulfilling career.

What I have seen over the years is people with passion for their job tend to outperform people with interest most every time. But you have to bring your talent too. Passion alone is not the key but it is important. I can be passionate about singing, but if I can't hold a tune, I'm going to sound passionately lousy. We see this happen watching the rejects performance from all those reality talent shows. Talent is the base denominator for greatness. What seems to be difficult for people to find is their passion. Or they really overlook it because others imprint on what they should be doing.

5

Recently I was watching an early morning show and the featured guest was from another country, and she was a southern soul food chef. Ok, this peaked my attention because I did not associate this country with southern soul food. You mean a person from down under cooks' southern soul food. I was highly skeptical. Ok I had conscious bias. But what really peeked my interest was how did she get to this point in her career. The host did an excellent job probing and asking all the right questions. So how did you become a chef? Well my father was a cook and owned his restaurant and I wanted to become a cook. However, my father discouraged me because he did not want me to work that hard and sacrifice time away from family, holidays and weekends. You see, owning a restaurant requires you to sacrifice a lot. So I went to college, then became a teacher. That didn't last long. Then I became a nurse. Quit that job too. I really wanted to cook, so, I did it! I started my own restaurant, and now, I'm here! Wow I thought! She followed her passion, but first listened to her father and tried to become something else. You have to listen to that inner voice and do what you love to do. Doing so puts you on a path of success. But getting to that point took her a decade and a half

I remember when I had the talk about career with my dad. As a teenager I played musical instruments, the saxophone, drums, and guitar. When it came time to declare what I was going to do, my dad asked me, "Do you think you can make more money as a musician, or an engineer?" Looking back at that conversation, I know now that I am no Maceo Parker (James Brown's saxophone player). I do have a passion for numbers and all things numbers. So I chose Mechanical Engineering as my starting point. But where we start our careers may not be where we land. Some of us will know early, some of us will find out twenty years later. And this is ok.

In this busy world we go about our daily lives not really paying attention to others while they work. I'm talking about the encounters you have with employees when you shop, purchase gas, food, entertainment etc. Can you tell if the person loves what they are doing, or are they miserable and plan to make your experience with them miserable too. Passion has an impact on a business. Finding the right fit for people to leverage their passion is important. We will discuss how to find your passion in chapter two.

So, what makes you happy? What brings you joy? I think answering these simple questions brings you closer to aligning your talent to your passion. One of my favorite quotes is by Walter Payton, *"When you are good at something, you will tell others. When you are great at something, they will tell you."* When passion is unleashed, greatness happens and others see you at your best, when your talent flourishes.

Chapter Two
Find Your Passion

Most of us have heard the phrase, "follow your passion." So are we supposed to have strong and uncontrollable emotion for our careers? First, passion is an important part of career success, but it is not the only thing we need to advance our careers. I believe you should love why you do what you do, if you don't, how can you bring your whole self to your career.

We will have a series of jobs throughout our lifetime, some jobs we will like, other jobs we will despise. Think of the job you have as WHAT you do, and your career as WHY you do what you do. Why do you do what you do? To help others? To build something new in a field of work? To drive innovation? To make as much money as you can? To be a CEO?

After having a series of jobs, you will find yourself at the end of a career. What will that day look like to you? Will you be fulfilled or will you have regrets? Each job you take is an important decision to how your career will end. Selecting the right job based on your development needs is an important part of the equation. But asking the question why am I about to take this job was more important. If I take this job, will it help me fulfill my Why? Why do I do what I do. Most important, does my WHY match up with my passion.

Is your WHY wrapped around making lots of money? Does money equal happiness for you? Money can do a lot of things and it can make dreams become fulfilled, and money can take dreams away. Chasing paper (money) has its place, but this is inherently challenging as a general strategy as money may lead many of us away from our true calling. So when you choose a career, don't be blinded by the money trail. Money can temporally make you happy, but no amount of money will buy happiness or time.

Living our lives to the fullest happens best when we are following our passion. However, let's face it, you may find yourself every week doing the 9 to 5 working a job you don't like to make money. This is no way for a person to live. Living this way is not sustainable for happiness nor success. When you are more passionate about the work you are doing, you truly enjoy what you do and you never really feel like work is work. When you are passionate about your work, you will be more engaged and have better ideas. In addition, you don't mind spending more time doing WHAT you do. People that love what they do go above and beyond what is asked of them in their job. No obstacle will stop a person with passion from achieving success. One person with passion, will beat 99 people without passion every time.

One of the most common obstacles in figuring out a passion-based career is determining what you're passionate about in the first place. We are taught to analyze things when we try to figure something out, But when you deal with a subject like passion, and try to figure it out, the process can be very difficult. We take tests, think about early childhood memories, ask relatives, mentors, friends, "What should I do?" The root cause here is passion can't be found in analysis (your head) because it is in your heart. In reality, no matter how hard you think about what is your passion, you won't figure it out. You need to follow your heart and feel your way to your truth, from the inside out.

Many years ago, I made a career change from engineering to training. I had a chance to conduct several training sessions and found I had more energy and excitement when I was involved in delivering and creating training programs. In fact, I looked forward to designing, developing and delivering training programs. General Electric was looking for a training manager to lead their new expansion through a state agency. I left a full-time job to peruse work as a contractor. The program was a success and a year later I was hired by the state agency as a full-time Training Specialist. Little did I know that this job was the first step me finding my passion. I did no analysis, I just did what made me fulfilled. I had to put in effective effort in my job and had to learn a great deal too. I knew nothing about building curriculum and training programs, but a man named Charlie took me under his tutelage and learned a great deal from him.

Passion. There are three things that must coexist in order for passion to be unleashed. First, you must like/love what you do (Enjoyment). Moving forward, if you don't like what you do, you could stop doing it, or love it with all your heart. Sounds easy right. I hate beets. So your saying I must love beets? No, "Bend your job until it breaks." Look for the nuggets in your job that will get you the development you need. If you are doing a job and don't know what you are getting out of it from a development perspective, then that is your answer. You are in the wrong job. If you can't change WHAT you are doing, you can change HOW you are doing it. Doing a job that you are not developing in is pure madness. We are creatures of habit and if you develop a bad habit of not seeking or getting development, a bad trend may occur that will hinder your career advancement. Don't expect to be miserable 80 percent of the day and happy and passionate in the last 20 percent. You have the power to control your own destiny and you are the master of your fate. The most successful people own their situation and drive their futures. Also, pay close attention to what you gravitate towards. What brings you the most happiness? How do you spend your time? What do you talk about? What books, movies, music do you spend your money on. Do you notice any themes? Remember, Walter Payton's quote. *"When you are good at something, you will tell others. When you are great at something, they will tell you."* What are you great at? Pay attention to compliments, and you may find yourself hearing the same compliment over and over again. People are describing your greatness. When your passion shows I bet your talent is close by. Remember, about following your heart, and not a formula.

Second, you must be good at what you do (Ability). Good performers are appreciated, great performers get noticed. You must be good or great at what you do. Performance is the entry ticket to play the game. We will find ourselves in jobs that will require us to learn a new skill, or develop a new competency. 70 percent of development will come from on the job activities. While 20 percent will come from coaches and 10 percent comes from traditional learning like classes, seminars, books etc. This is known as the 70-20-10 concept of development. You should always have a development plan that is linked to improving your knowledge, skill, or ability.

Finally, the organization must value what you do (Relevant). Don't fall victim to nobody feels my job is important. Or my boss does not understand what I do or what my team does. Bend your job until it breaks. In other word, flip the situation. If you feel the organization does not put any relevance in what you do, educate them! Show why WHAT you do is important. Take control of the situation rather than sit back.

When you are in your sweet spot, and your passion is unleashed most of the time you are unstoppable. Remember passion is important, but it is not the only thing you must bring to your career. Passion without bringing your talent along could look pretty bad.

Have you ever watched a talent show where a person comes on stage in front of the judges and proclaims that they will sing a song. Judges say, proceed, and then it happens, the most horrendous sound comes out of the contestants mouth as they butcher the song. Everyone starts making faces, the contestant gets booed, and removed from the stage. Now mind you, the contestant performing did their performance with great passion. After all, they had barely uncontrollable emotion when they were singing. But here is the deal with the singer. The person had no talent for singing. Talent is the foundation and we get better when we put in effective effort around honing our knowledge, skills, and abilities.

The same thing happens in careers too. People align a career without considering if the job leverages their talent. No matter how hard you work on developing something that is not in your natural DNA, you will not succeed. For example, for the most part, if you are a left-handed pitcher and a great one at that, why would you practice pitching with your right hand? Focus your development on your strengths. Your strengths come from a foundation of your talent. Your talent gets better with effective effort applied to developing your knowledge, skills, and abilities.

Your talent is what got you here, and your talent is what will get you there! Build on what you are great at and your superpowers will be unleashed. And if you happen to love what you are doing too, look out there is no stopping you!

Chapter Three
Leveraging Your Strengths & Talents

If your company mission is to climb trees, which would you rather do: Hire a squirrel, or train a horse? Understanding your strengths is very important when considering your development and career advancement. Consider the skills of a squirrel and horse. The squirrel has the skills and talent to climb a tree with very little effort. On the other hand, no matter how much our friend the horse tries, it may never make it up the tree. Passion for climbing trees won't help our friend the horse, nor any amount of training will help.

To make sure you are maximizing your development, understand your strengths and find roles that will allow your talents to flourish. Self-awareness is extremely important, and when it comes to understanding your strengths, I highly recommend taking the Gallup Strength Finders assessment. By the way, my top five strengths are, *Relator, Restorative, Context, Learner, and Input.*

My Top 5 Strengths

Relator	People who are strong in the relator theme enjoy close relationships with others. They find deep satisfaction in working hard with friends to achieve a goal.
Restorative	People strong in restorative theme are adept at dealing with problems. They are good at figuring what is wrong and resolving it.
Context	People strong in the context theme enjoy thinking about the past. They understand the present by researching the past.
Learner	People strong in the Learner theme have a great desire to learn and want to continuously improve. In particular, the process of learning, rather than the outcome, excites them/.
Input	People strong in the Input theme have a craving to know more. Often they like to collect and archive all kinds of information.

Regarding my Relator theme, I do have close friends that I keep up with even for decades. As a six sigma black belt I really like fixing processes and problems that require statistical analysis to determine the direction or solution to follow. You get to define, measure, analyze, improve and control processes. In HR you get to fix processes and people stuff. I can watch the history channel all weekend long! I may sprinkle in the show "How it's Made," to round off my viewing. I find these types of television shows really exciting! As a learner, I was the kid that looked through the entire encyclopedia because of curiosity. Now I just surf the internet, but have to make sure what I am reading is factual. Many times I will do more research when necessary. Input. I have over 3,000 DVD/Blue Ray movies, and I have watched many of them several times. Yeah I could do the fancy streaming, but 7,000 movies away from my goal of 10,000. No not really! But I do have some old floppy disk from many years back. The big floppies. The point here is after I took the strength finders assessment it gave me additional insight into how I tick. I know what types of roles I would thrive in and the types that I would really suck at. The great thing in my current role and with my current leader, is she understands my strengths and aligns my work to my strengths. Great leaders know how to maximize your talent and strengths. If you find yourself in a position where your manager does not know how to leverage your talent and strengths, remember the concept of bending your job until it breaks.

Did you know that Walt Disney was a lousy artist? Walt Disney failed many times in his early career. However, Walt Disney became self-aware of his lack of ability when it came to drawing so he surrounded himself with great a artist. The newly acquired artist was able to take the brilliant ideas Walt had and turned them into animations. Thankful Walt Disney was able to capitalize on his strengths. Now many decades later, his legacy is still with us.

What is talent? A talent is a recurring pattern of thought, feeling or behavior that can be effectively applied. Every job performed at excellence requires talent. A talent shows up as something that happens often and naturally. Think of a talent as a four lane superhighway of the mind. Then there are the back roads. What is a strength? A strength is the ability to provide consistent, near-perfect performance in a given activity.

When you think about famous people, either current or historical figures. When you look at their accomplishments and take a closer look at how they developed their knowledge, skills and abilities into what made them great at what they do, you will always find a talent.

For example, being drawn towards meeting new people and enjoying the opportunity of making a connection with them are talents associated with the Woo strength finders theme, whereas the ability to consistently build a network of supporters who know you and are prepared to aid you is a strength. In order to build a strength, you must improve your talents with skills and knowledge.

Skills, talents, and knowledge are each important for building a strength, talent is always the most important. The reason is your talents are innate and cannot be acquired, unlike skills and knowledge. For example, as a customer service representative you can learn your product services (knowledge), you can be trained to ask the right open-ended questions (a skill), and you can practice making a connection (investment). However, the innate tendency to push a customer to commit at the right moment, in the right way must be naturally occurring and cannot be learned.

I remember going out for the varsity basketball team in high school and I made it through one team practice. One thing I could do really good was jump I mean jump really high for a six foot lanky teenager. My nickname was Frog because I could jump really high. So, I thought, hey try out for the basketball team! Well, during a drill where you were to be looking for a ball being passed to you, well I was not looking and got drilled right in the side of the head! Down I went! Nevertheless, coach said. "Cohen, you should think about being my team statistician, I hear you are good at math." There it is again, that math thing. Well coach was right, and I was unaware of my strengths at the time. I never became team statistician either because I was too embarrassed by getting hit. Maybe I missed a great opportunity by not taking the feedback. After all, coach was a legend in the area and recognized as one of the best basketball coaches. I'm sure coach could have taught me a lot, but I missed out on the development opportunity because I did not listen to coaches feedback.

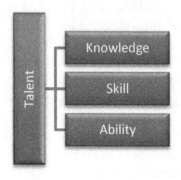

Chapter Four
The Journey

The lack of having a vision will lead to an unfulfilled career. A clear idea of where you want to be in a few months or years and **why** – is a crucial part of developing your purpose. Your vision is your guide to developing your personal strategy. It helps you to ensure that **what you do** gets you **where you want to be**. As you embark on your journey, two things will be of upmost importance. First, it will be important to have a vision regarding where your career is heading. For some people this will come easy, and for others, it may take a decade or two to figure out. Either way, you must look ahead. Next, you must have a plan to support your vision. Some people say you don't need a plan, but I disagree with their approach or lack of having one. It helps to know where you are going, and how you will get there.

Think of your career as a journey. Webster defines a journey as an act of traveling one place to another, usually taking a rather long time. Chances are you have used a GPS to get directions for a long trip, and even a short trip as well. With your GPS or SERI (Special Education Resources on the Internet) most of us have a sense of comfort knowing we are making the right turns when on our journey. After all, if you make a wrong turn, you get the "Rerouting" voice message, then "recalculating new route" message. We get a lot of help from technology these days to help us navigate where we are going. But how much help do we get or seek when it comes to navigating our career choices?

Just like taking a long trip, our careers take shape one job after another job and so on, with the hope we will end in the right job that springs a career. So let's say you get on a plane, settle into your seat, and the pilot says welcome to flight 006. Our flight time this evening will be 7 hours and 3 minutes. We will have you in Dallas in no time. But wait! You are going to Los Angeles! How did this happen! How did I make it past all the checks and re-checks to end up on the wrong plane! The plane door closes. You panic. And now you are on your way to the wrong destination.

Now what I just described pretty much won't happen, but I've seen many employees not have a written plan or goal regarding their career. In fact only 1% of employees have written goals regarding their career. So how are the 99% navigating towards their career goals? How do they know they are selecting the right job that will give them maximum development. Sometimes luck is in your favor, sometimes you are in the right place in the right time. But given the amount of time and energy we put into our careers, why leave it to chance?

When developing your vision, consider five key things:

1. Develop a Personal Vision
2. Refine and Narrow Your Vision
3. Set Personal Goals
4. Have a Career Board of Directors

5. Vision Boards are Helpful

Develop your personal vision by knowing what success looks like for you both in the short and long terms. Consider all aspects of your life because you will need balance. This could be ensuring you have time for family, friends, hobbies, health activities and spiritual balance. There will be give and take required from you when trying to figure the right balance. And you may consider making a career change to strike the right balance in your life. So when you glance into the long term future (ten years out), and see yourself at your destination, know that you will need to make trade-offs along the way. In the short term, think about the things you need to get done in order to reach the ten year mark.

Once you have your vision formed, create a vision board. A vision board is a collage of pictures that represent your journey towards your vision. Why would you want to make such a board? Having a visual picture placed in your home that you will see daily, will remind you of the mission you are on. Why do you do what you do on a daily basis to push forward towards a series of goals? A vision board helps remind you of your future. I've seen where vision board parties are held where several people come together and create their vision boards. After their masterpieces are done, they are shared with the group. Several things happen at such a party. First you find yourself surrounded by likeminded successful people on missions and you may meet an accountability buddy. Vision boards are good to share with mentors too. We all get bogged down in the day to day, and having a small reminder of where you are going can help keep you focused on the end game.

I am a Saint Louis Business Diversity Initiative Fellow and graduated from cohort nine. Many of my cohort fellows created vision boards, and I have seen and tracked many blossoming careers. I've witnessed firsthand that having a plan works, and having a vision gets you moving towards what you want. We plan the simple things in life like meals, what type of car to buy, or your holiday shopping list. Do you have a career plan? Written goals to cover the short term activities? Visual representation of your goals? It's more than saying I want to be a (fill in here) by (this date). One final comment regarding vision boards. The vision board should be representative of your whole plan, that includes but not limited to your personal, wellbeing, career, family and spiritual goals.

Do you have a career board of directors? Trusted Advisors, Mentors, and Coaches. As you plan your career, and select jobs that will give you the maximum development, it is good to have people you trust give you advice. A mentor, is someone that can help you think your job selections as you progress in your career. A coach is someone that can help you develop a specific gap that needs to be filled in order for you to advance your career. Coaches provide direction when you are improving a competency, or gaining knowledge, or improving a skill or ability. You are the CEO of your career, so get a board of directors if you don't have one. Having different perspectives from people that will guide you in the right direction rather than telling you what you want to hear will serve you well.

You have to know what you need to improve on to achieve a particular ambition, and then work on it. I call this place "Delta" or the gap you need to close. This is where self-awareness is critical. You must be really honest about knowing your opportunities for development. In most cases, a person will need to improve a competency, or improve their knowledge, skill or ability. Once you have listed the things you need to develop in, prioritize your list from importance to essential. Start by:

- Listing all development areas: Then ask…
- How important is this to me? (1-5)
- 1 = Low importance
- 5 = High importance
- How essential is it to develop now? (1-5)
- 1 = Not that important
- 5 = Extremely important
- Add together the scores
- Examine the top three scores and plan your development around the most important and essential areas.

Example

Area to Develop	Type of Development	Import-ance	Essent-ial	Total
Leadership	Competency	5	4	9
Organizationa l Skills	Skill	2	1	4
Effective listening	Skill	3	3	6
Business Acumen	Competency	5	5	10
Teamwork skills	Skill	2	3	5
Decision Analytics	Competency	3	3	6
Influencing	Competency	3	5	8

Example above top three in ranked order:

1. Business Acumen
2. Leadership
3. Influencing

The delta in the example above directs you to complete a comprehensive individual development plan around three competencies, Business Acumen, Leadership, and Influencing.

Example Individual Development Plan

We will come back to your IDP (Individual Development Plan) in chapter six, and discuss why the IDP is critical when selecting the right job during job changes. In addition, Write S.M.A.R.T goals to hold yourself accountable. SMART goals are Specific, Measurable, Attainable, Relevant, and Time Bound.

SMART Goal Example

I will improve my health by eating 60 grams of protein and drinking 2 liters of water every day.

For me, the most frustrating thing as a Human Resources professional is when someone seeks career advice from me and has no idea where they are going. No development plan in mind too. I get it, there are those times this should happen, like early in your career. But having a little idea of where your passion lies, and how your talents are being used is a great starting point. Begin with the end in mind. What do you see yourself doing at the end of your career? Does your dream career match up with your passion? Does it leverage your talent? Is it realistic? And can you close your opportunities through development.

Chapter Five
The 5 Stages of a Career

Consider your career as a professional basketball game. Within the basketball game, there are four quarters, a halftime, timeouts, and maybe an overtime. Let's say each quarter represents ten years of your career. So, you have forty years on average to complete your career. Some of us will work longer, others will have shorter careers and enter retirement sooner. Either way, we all go through the 5 stages if we have a fulfilled career. The five stages of a career are:

1. Exploration
2. Establishment
3. Mid-Career
4. Late Career
5. Legacy

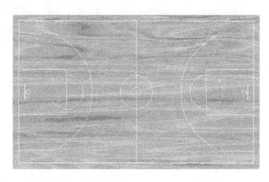

Which quarter are you in? Early? Late? On your way to Legacy? I think it's important to put your career into a timeframe. If you are in the Early career stage you have plenty of runway (time) to advance. The closer you get to the Legacy stage, the shorter your runway. Within a ten year time frame, you could potentially have two to three key jobs. Every job you take counts, so make the right choices! There is nothing worse than doing a job that does not count towards your development. If you are not developing, you are wasting time, and time is not on your side. Before you know it, you are at halftime (20 years into the game).

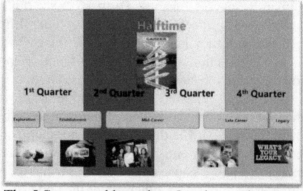

The 5 Stages and how they Overlap each Quarter

Exploration: Happens during the first moments of the first quarter, and is the period in our career that we start to think about WHAT we want to do. This time is marked by selecting a university or trade school to attend. Or some go straight into the workforce. There are decisions to make, and sometimes pressure from family and friends to declare a major. Or, you are told you will be a lawyer, doctor, engineer, scientist, mechanic like another family member. Most of the time many people have an idea about WHAT they want to do but are not really one hundred percent sure. Nevertheless, people feel compelled to get started. Do something with your life! Don't just mosey around, go do something! Many high school graduates get the nudge to get moving. So we move.

What's funny to me is and I have seen this a lot. Ask someone with at least 15 years of experience, "What field of study is their degree in?" Then ask them, "What do you do? You might hear things like, "My degree is in Finance, but I'm a Supply Chain Director. Or, "I have my B.S in IT, but I'm a Sr. Human Resources Business Partner." I see it a lot in resumes, where people have careers entirely different than the path they landed on. Why is this? Why the change in direction? After all, a lot of work went into preparing for the start. During the Exploration Phase we get started, but may find out within a few years, after we press the start button, we are not so enthused about our job. Maybe the passion is not there, or that feeling of satisfaction is not there. Or, we are just not good at what we chose to do. Some people drop out of the university scene, others enter the university at a later start date. For most, we need to feel our way to find our job that meets what we like. For many during this phase, some key drivers that influence which job we take are, money, location, title, company, perks etc. But none of the things I mentioned help you figure out WHAT you need to do in order to close your delta (development gap). For the lucky few, you may get selected to enter into a management rotational program, or internship. Not so lucky if you planned to be an intern or go into a management rotational program from the start.

Some people enter into the Exploration Phase knowing exactly what they will do in life and their end game figured out. They get a running start at their career and sometimes referred to as prodigies, or serious minded. If a parent wants a child to be a concert pianist, and pays for piano lessons and the child attends recitals and has completed hours upon hours of practice time, and then one day, says to the parent, "I don't want to play the piano anymore!" Your passion is not transferable. You cannot imprint passion onto a child, yes the child had interest in playing the piano, but when the time came to inform the parent of their true passion, well let's just say, we are at a crossroad.

Scenes like what I just described play out during the Exploration Phase. Now there are times when a child's interest turns out to be their passion, and when their talents are developed and their knowledge, skills, and abilities naturally accelerate, you get the likes of Janet Jackson, Tiger Woods, Stevie Wonder, and Steve Jobs. Coaching and Mentoring can pay off when done in the right way during development at an early age. The William sisters are a great example of passion and dedication to developing your knowledge within your field and near perfect development of skills. The talent for tennis was there, the passion for the game was there, and excellent coaching and mentorship provided excellent insight. The good news is you have time to make decisions, change your mind and hit the career reset button. Most people press the career reset button at some point within the first ten years of their career. I did. From mechanical engineering to training.

Establishment Phase: The main activity during the Establishment Phase is centered around developing your foundation. You have pressed the career start button, and there is a lot to learn. During this phase it is important to focus on performance. Because performance is the entry ticket to play the game. What game? The upward mobility game. People that perform get recognized. People that get recognized get discussed amongst leaders. And when leaders know you, that is a good thing. Actually it is great exposure. When leaders recognize your potential, they tend to invest in your development, and sponsor you for new opportunities. What starts to take shape is your image, or brand. Your brand is your calling card. Your brand is what you are known for within the organization. Many times what you are known for is linked to your talent and passion.

We gain much needed experience during the Establishment Phase. Technical knowledge, functional skills, and key functional competencies tend to dominate the development plans. Personally, I stumbled my why through the Establishment Phase. During the first 9 years of my career I wanted to be a Mechanical Engineer. Right out the gate, my first job was Management Trainee for the largest textile company in the world at that time. That company was on a major decline and I did not know it because I didn't do my research on the company. I just wanted a job! After all, we were in a recession, and felt lucky to even have a job. What I did promise myself after leaving my first job was I would make sure I only worked for the best companies that invested in capital, people, and had new products being introduced into the market. I felt if a company was investing in capital and people with a drive towards innovation, I would be able to build the skills and gain experience to help me compete and develop. I lucked into some great jobs the next decade but what I did do right was I kept adding new skills/competencies to my tool belt. Training & Development, Process Engineering, Design of Experiments, Statistical Process Control, to list a few early things.

I worked hard. Really hard, but made slow upward progress. I approached work in a very competitive way. I was a poor teammate, it was all about me, I had a temper, and I really did not care how other people at work felt. The quality of my work was excellent, so I feel my supervisors and managers tolerated me. Looking back, most did not give me career advice, or share any insights. Until I ran into a gentleman named Joe Raines. Joe worked for Black & Decker in a different division than the one I worked in. Once a year Joe would contact me and check in to see how I was doing. For about three years I got the yearly call from Joe, but one time he was looking for a Training and Safety Manager for a division of Textron. At the time, I was working for a division of Sara Lee as the Corporate Manager of Training & Development. Did you notice the names of the companies. Black & Decker, Sara Lee, Textron. These were all heavyweights in their respective sectors. I was keeping my promise to work with great organizations. Well it turns out I took the job working for Joe. During the next five years Joe worked on me (coached/mentored) and when I emerged, I was a different person. I approached work as a team player concerned about helping others. What is in it for you? The more I shared, the more others shared. Many opportunities were brought my way. Actually, it was when my potential really came to the forefront. A few tools I picked up along the way were, Certified ISO9001 Lead Auditor, Certified ISO14001 Lead Auditor, VPP (Voluntary Protection Program) Lead, Six Sigma/Lean Black Belt Certification, and I finally completed a B.S. in Business Administration. I often tell people I was a late bloomer. Well, it took me until halftime of my career to realize what I wanted to be. I wanted to be an HR Director. At this point in my career, I had training and safety experience. I needed to make another turn in order to get where I wanted to go. But now, I know where I am headed. I know what I need to develop too. Opportunity came quickly. Goodbye Michigan, hello Mississippi. HR Manger job with Textron, and it is leading the HR team at a major plant startup.

Mid-Career: So you want to be in HR I thought. People like to bring their problems to HR. Well, Human Resources backwards is resource for humans. Talent Management, Compensation, Employee Relations, Talent Acquisition, Employment Law, Coaching and Development to mention a few things I had to come up to speed on. Yes, On-the-job training. A sponsor took a chance on me, and I had to deliver. I loved the challenge, I really liked seeing people develop. But there were parts of the job that were painful but required me to hone my skills. Terminations, investigations, conflict resolutions and on and on. I got good at my job because of effective effort. Sometimes I felt great with how my skills were coming along regarding my development.

Mid-career is demanding because at this point you may be not only responsible for yourself, you may be leading a small team, site, division or region. Leading people requires a whole new set of skills and competencies. Just because you might be an excellent individual contributor does not make you the best leader of people. I have seen this play out many times. A person comes into my office and declares they want to lead a team. I guess people think they have to lead people to make more money or to get promoted. Which is not the case. Only to find out they hate the work that comes with leading a team, and they fail miserably. They tap out.

Mid-career comes along when mid-life is happening too. Maybe you are on your second marriage, or you may have children starting their university education or leaving the house to master a frontier. Empty nest. Do I really want to pursue that corner office? I don't feel like moving again. Lots of things seem to enter the equation and sometimes makes people reconfigure the outcome. Nevertheless, Mid-Career comes with many rewards too. Experience has its advantages and great companies look for strong leaders and innovators.

Your LinkedIn page gets many views from recruiters trying to steal you away from the company you work for. If your image (brand) is right and it matches your experience, recruiters both internally and externally will seek you out. You are known within the industry, or company for something and you are building towards having a legacy.

During a time early in my career, I went on an interview for a mechanical draftsman role. I went to the interview dressed in gray MC Hammer pants! I'm not kidding. You don't know what you don't know. Red shoes and a red shirt too. You see, me and my buddy were going out to party that night, so I wore my party clothes to the interview. Well, needless to say, I did not get the job. Guess my image did not match their corporate environment. I looked good on paper (resume). You might be thinking, they should have been more inclusive. Diversity and Inclusion were not common themes back then in the corporate world. You want to be a leader, dress like one, lead like one, behave like one, yet be yourself too.

Leaders tend to see your potential before you do. Those leaders will become your sponsors. Everyone has had someone take a chance on them. When those moments happen, take advantage of them. In the meantime, prepare as if that day is coming tomorrow.

Late Career: About fifteen years prior to you retiring, you enter the late in career phase. You may find yourself deep into your dream career, leading large organizations, companies, or have that extensive experience in your field or craft. You are a trusted leader that is not only leading, are preparing the future of the company/organization as well. You may find yourself at the top of where you planned to be.

That's good, but you must stay current or the world will pass you by.

One of the most challenging things for me is dealing with people that have unfulfilled career dreams in late career. There is only so many CEO, Sr. VP, VP, Sr. Dir roles at the top of an organization. When succession plan discussions occur, and organizations select who will lead the few key top roles, you see good talent beat out by great talent. In cases, people may feel their trajectory is still upward, but in reality, their career has plateaued. And the critical conversation about career trajectory does not happen, leaving people very disappointed when they are passed over for that final big opportunity. But self-awareness and conducting an assessment of your potential will prepare you for that day, should it come, when you know you have maxed out your potential.

I have seen experienced employees transfer knowledge and experience at a rapid pace during their late career phase, thus bringing their value to the organization exponentially. You may find yourself working for someone that once worked for you. I have even told high potential HR talent that have worked for me, that one day they could be my boss. They give me a strange look, but I was thinking, I see your potential. My thought regarding the Late Career Phase is, finish strong!

Legacy: As you wind down your career, hopefully you have built a legacy and people will be talking about what you have done, long after you leave the organization. By now hopefully you will have had a series of jobs that you developed or elevated new competencies/skills/abilities in each role. Your passion has shown through and your talent has been leveraged. You can clearly see what you have built, the people you have helped, and organizations that benefited from your presence.

Many of us have heard of the Hall of Fame. Many sports organizations use the Hall of Fame to recognize the best of the best in their sport. Companies, Federal and State Agencies etc. do the same thing too. Organizations recognize lifetime achievement, 40 Under 40, 30 under 30, Person of the Year. G.O.A.T (Greatest of All Time). Michael Jordon for basketball, and Tom Brady for football. What did Muhammad Ali say, "I am the greatest!", And Ali was and still is. We all will leave an impression on someone we have encountered through our career, and may be consider a G.O.A.T in the minds of those encountered. On the flip side, your retirement party might be unattended and you are forgotten the day you leave.

I had a coworker that I worked with for ten years. It just happened that we worked in the same department for the last two years of his career. This gentleman was the most experienced Human Resources Lead in Human Resources. At 4:30 PM on his final day at work, he never stopped doing what he did best. My nickname for him is Machine. Why Machine? The amount of quality HR coverage and advice he could do was amazing. He operated at full speed ahead in the right thoughtful way. I thought, I hope I am as energized as Machine is on my last day.

Well if you love what you do, it does not feel like work.

Overtime: The fourth quarter is complete and you enter into overtime. Retirement. But you don't stop sharing your talent. You have more time to give back, or start a new career. Forty years will come and go fast so make the best of your time. Be sure to take time outs along the way to recharge yourself and reflect.

Chapter Six
Select the Right Job

Career satisfaction does not come from what you do, but from who you get to be while doing it. And who you get to be is the real you. I didn't like every job in my career, nor did I make the right decision when selecting each job I held. However, I was I able to be myself in each job and that was fulfilling.

Now let's focus on the Future State which is about looking forward. Or what I call the role you seek. The problem I see most people make is that they concentrate on the next role without thinking critically about several roles into the future. Once you know your gap, then you should focus on honing in on that Future State role.

Harvey Coleman, the originator of the P.I.E. concept laid it out well. Performance, Image, Exposure. Future State is about Image and Exposure. Remember, Performance gets you noticed by leaders. If you know you want to be a Finance Director, but you are currently two or more roles away from the role, Exposure to key individuals in leadership will be required. Formulating the right Image is important too. Again, Image is about your reputation, your brand.

The key is to maximize your development in whatever role you take. After you accept the job, and someone asks you, "Why did you take that role?" You should have an answer and it should be tied to your development. If you can't answer that question, you may have taken the wrong job.

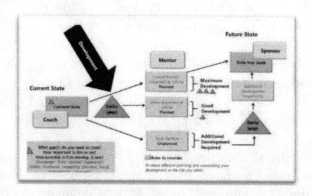

However, if you can articulate why you took the job, and explain what you are getting out of the role, and how this role will help you land "X" in the future, you are closer to building a good Individual Development Plan (IDP)..

When you are in a period of assessment and transition, consider the following questions:

- Why are you in your current job?
- Why did you select the company? Their mission? Brand? Leader in the industry?
- How many development items will you cover while in the role you selected? 1? 2? 3?
- What investments does the company you work for or are moving to do around community involvement, capital, employee development?

- Does the company have Inclusion and Diversity as a main pillar?
- Did you look at the company website? What did you see? Diversity? Lack of Diversity? Are all the corporate leaders the majority of one gender?
- How strong is the company's performance?
- Did you read the investor communications? What is going on within the company? Or they may not be traded on Wall Street. Does that matter to you?
- How has this company been recognized? Best Company to Work for list? Forbes 100 list? etc.

So why all the questions Dan? Well, if you are going to make a move to another company, or join a company, you are entrusting that company to help you, move your career in the direction you are striving. If the new company does not meet your development needs, then you will waste valuable time.

When you work for the best companies, you have better odds of receiving the best development. Therefore, you should be very selective when choosing a company to join. The company mission is important. When looking into joining a company, really look at the website as it contains a plethora of information. The company mission is important and see if their mission resonates with you and your beliefs. If the mission does, your passion for the work you do will come easier. You have a purpose when you get up each morning. Examine the executive leadership team and read their profiles. Is the executive leadership team diverse? If yes, you may see more diversity deeper in the organization too.

Consider the products the company makes. Are their blockbuster products on the downside of the product life cycle? Is the company investing in new products to deliver to their markets. A great company will innovate and invest in new product offerings. Great companies tend to invest in their employees development too. The great companies land on all the Best Places to Work lists for Innovation, Diversity, IT, Technology, Family, etc. A company that has a culture supporting development is one worth joining.

I have worked for a bad company, many good companies, and one great company. Thankfully, the great company I worked for taught me how to manage my development. I did ok for the first twenty years, and through luck, great leaders looked out for me and my mentor got me on track really fast.

At the end of the day, ask yourself, did I develop today? Each year you should see exponential growth as you gain experience. During my time at the bad company was hate my job, despised my bad boss and look for ways to get out of his department. I dreaded going to work. One day I walked in and quit. I had a job though. Interviewed on a Saturday, was at work that Monday. It felt good quitting that horrible job. During this period in my life, I learned one valuable lesson, and that is, "I control my career fate!" You don't have to stay in a job you hate. Nothing good ever comes from that.

While working for the many good companies, I got to do things I loved doing! I had great role models, coaches, and life was good! I saw the impact I was making in my field of work. Leaders were pulling me along and sponsoring me for other roles even when I did not know until after I got the job. You see, someone will always take a chance on you when you show up as YOU. What I mean by this is, your strengths and talent show through when your A game is on.

With the great company I developed more in the first ten years than my previous twenty years. The development was intentional. The people leaders I worked for took great care in making sure I had a sound individual development plan that we discussed often. My NPA (Next Planned Assignment) was discussed too based on my interest, development needs, and talent. I knew when I entered a job, what my development was, and what success looked like when completed. If you are in a job right now, and you don't know what you are developing and what success looks like, reassess and find out now. If you don't know what your development is, how do you determine if the work you are doing now will get you where you are going. You are traveling without a destination.

In surveying the response of hundreds of participants in six studies, the researchers found that, when asked to name their single biggest regret in life, 76 percent of participants gave one top answer: they didn't fulfill their ideal self.

We may have a flawed attitude toward how we avoid regret. We live in a world in which we are told that we'll have a wonderful life if we follow the rules.. Work hard and you will get ahead. Keep your head down and don't make trouble. It's not what you know but who you know (Don't be fooled, you need to know your field).

So you figure that if you do all the things society expects of you – be good, get married at the appropriate time, make enough money to pay the bills -you'll feel. Maybe not.

Career satisfaction does not come from what you do, but from who you get to be while doing it. And who you get to be is the real you.

Chapter Seven
Be Ready Enough

We are never completely ready for anything; we just have to be ready enough. Society puts a lot of pressure on us to always be ready. Almost every hour of the day we are with ads and marketing on TV, radio, internet, newspaper, billboards etc. Most are about being ready for something. You need more insurance because you are getting older, you need this supplement because of X, you need to eat this because of that.

Accept the fact that being ready enough is ok. Think back to each job you have held. Did you know everything about that job on your first day? Do you still have the same day-one fear about not being ready enough when you started the job? You were hired so believe me, you were ready enough. Most employers won't pay you money or hire you if they did not think you were going to help the company cause.

Seventy percent of what you learn is through experience. Most people get experience by doing. But be ready enough to compete for the job and get through a successful interview. Be ready enough to start your business. Or wherever your passion and talent leads you. To be ready enough is good enough to keep your career progressing.

Ready enough here you come. We may not always be ready but we can at least bring a raincoat or umbrella. Preparing to be ready enough comes back to working on the right development. Understanding what is the right development for you has to come from self-awareness. A coach can help you work on the development, and mentor can help you think through how the development can help your career. And finally a sponsor will help open the doors for new opportunities. But you have to be ready enough, which is seen by others as potential.

But Dan, raindrops keep falling on my head, because I didn't see the storm coming. The storm being the perceived obstacles in your way. But if you are focusing on the right development, you can fall back on knowledge, skill, and ability to get you through. The only thing that holds you back from achieving your dream career is you. Fear, doubt, comfort are a few barriers, but they can be overcome.

If your performance has been effective and leaders in the organization notice you because of great performance, you have entered the game. Great performance gets noticed all the time, not only from leaders within your organization but leaders outside your organization too. Along with performance you need to have the right image as well. Lead, perform, act and dress the part before you get the part. You must cultivate the right image in order to your performance. Your brand is extremely important when sponsors consider giving a helping hand. After all, it is the sponsor who is putting their reputation on the line when they bring you forward to consideration. In addition, and probably the most important thing regarding being ready enough is exposure. Who in the leadership side of the organization knows you?   You must connect with leaders and tell them your career aspirations, what you are doing about your development, and please make sure the role you are currently in is part of your development.

When the time comes, and it will come, a sponsor will put your name forward for a role. You will be asked to participate in the interview process, or the job may be offered to you outright. Either way, be ready to accept the role even if it terrifies you. What you don't know is a gap, and gap that can be closed by development in the new role. Often times people do a role too long hoping that they will be better prepared for the next role. Wasted time! Know there is a balance that must be found too. You don't want to rush from one job to the next either. You really have to enter the role with an understanding of what development opportunities you are trying to accomplish while doing this role. Also, know what successful development looks like once you have finished your development goals. Then and only then should you look for the next opportunity. I have seen people get into a role without an understanding of what and why, only to be asking the organization in less than a year can they move to another role. This kind of quick movement without full development only hurts a person's image or brand. If you can't master your own development, how can you manage as a leader other's development.

During the second quarter of my career, I was doing a Training Specialist role at Black & Decker company, and I really wanted to break into the training manager realm. One day I received a call from a recruiter looking for a Corporate Training Manager, and guess what! The job was located in my home town. I went through the interview process, and nailed the interview I might say, and on my way home, got a call, and a job offer. Now I had to let my manager and company know that I would be taking this job with another company. I remember telling my boss Cindy, and she said, "I thought you would get that job! "I gave them your name!" Cindy was all smiles and happy for me. My, boss was my sponsor and I did not even know it. What Cindy knew was, I was ready enough for the next level.

Your next opportunity can come from any direction, so be ready enough. So I went to PYA Monarch, a division of Sara Lee Corporation as Corporate Training & Development Manager. I really learned a lot in this job, made many mistakes too, but my boss stuck in there with me. I learned about leadership competencies, succession planning, talent management and leadership development programs. The corporate world was much different than the manufacturing plant world. Politics, strategy, and the complexity of the work was at a different level and pace.

This role was awesome in terms of seeing how high potential leaders get developed and you see some make it, while others fall along the wayside. Those that did not excel did several things, one either they stopped developing, or two, played the game wrong and stopped developing. Sometime political job suicide did leaders in. If you focus too much on exposure and not enough on performance, it will hurt your image. Top performers got talked about during succession planning. And for the most part, they got the open VP and President roles.

While at PYA Monarch, my boss the VP of Human Resources said, "Cohen, you will be a VP of HR one day." I never saw that one coming. My boss saw something in me that I did not see in myself. Three years into my job at PYA Monarch, I got a call from Joe Raines, who worked at Black & Decker several years when I was there. This year, Joe would call me and see how I was doing. However, this time Joe called me with a job opportunity. Training & Safety Manager for a division of Textron. I went for the interview got the job and spent the next nine years of my career with Textron. I was ready enough to take on a new area called ES&H, Environmental Health & Safety. Let me tell you, I had no idea about EH&S, but Joe felt I could do the job. Fast forward 5 years later, and my site was the first within Textron to achieve the OSHA VPP (Voluntary Protection Program) Star, and first to achieve ISO 14001 certification. These were major accomplishments. This role helped me learn how to manage projects and lead teams that did not even directly report into me.

It was during my first five years with Textron that Joe Raines became my mentor. In fact, Joe was a coach, mentor, and sponsor. I was in the second quarter of my career and wanted to enter into the HR world as a career. I wanted to be an HR Manger. I was not ready. Not ready at ALL for a Human Recourses job. But Joe worked on me, and I was a hard case according to Joe. I recently had dinner with Joe and his wife Marylyn over Christmas break, and

Joe said, "Dan, you were my toughest case." "Well, look at you now, you have traveled the world, and you are developing others." "I'm proud of you."

Sponsors saw something in me well before I saw it in myself. But what I did do well was perform. I made sure I delivered high quality programs in everything I delivered. I made sure my bosses looked good. I kept my bosses boss off my bosses back, which is the first rule of corporate survival. When you are least expected, a sponsor will tap you on the shoulder and present you with a development opportunity. Joe is an exceptional coach too. Joe helped me develop the skills I needed to be in HR.

I had to move to Detroit for my next opportunity, and like the others, I was asked through nomination (Sponsor) to be in the 11th wave of Textron's Six Sigma Black Belt program. This was a great opportunity, but I was stepping out of the HR function to go into the Six Sigma organization. Mostly everyone else in my cohort were engineers, accountants, operations managers etc. I definitely did not feel ready for this role, but I could not say no.

The next two years were hard being a southern boy living in the frozen tundra, but I survived. Finished my black belt certification and then asked to lead the new greenfield startup in Greenville, Mississippi as HR Manager. Finally, I am an HR Manager and I just stepped into halftime of my career. I'm sure the company was happy I asked to move to Greenville, Mississippi, because no other takers stepped forward. Well, I ran back south as quickly as I could! I built my HR team, and they were good. As a new people leader I had things to learn, and as a Human

Resources Business Partner, I really had to learn how to influence.

The Greenfield project was a disaster. Let's just say I gained a lot of weight due to stress. I was 366 pounds and one step away from falling into a grave. Started up a 500 employee plant, and within a year shutdown the plant because of many, I mean many issues. But looking back, I learned more about what not to do during times that have dysfunction at the center of the storm, and how to lead and stick to what you believe as a leader.

Small town to an even smaller town. I changed roles, this time I went to Delta & Pine Land in Scott, Mississippi. Five hundred employees and I'm their new HR Director. Best decision of my professional career at the time. I was ready enough, and had a lot of things I would and did bring to the role. Leadership development program, compensation review for hourly employees, and rebranding the HR Team. I had the freedom to do really cool things even present to the Board of Directors.

Then it happened, and it was out of all of our hands and control. We were bought by a Fortune 100 company for 1.6 billion dollars. Little did I know, that my career development would speed up tenfold by joining this company. You see, development of employees was truly at the center of every leaders job. Ready or not, be ready enough.

Chapter Eight
Develop or Become Obsolete

Dissatisfaction is the base for progress, once you become satisfied, you become obsolete. Never stop developing, never stop learning. The single most devastating thing that will derail a career is to stop developing. I had a person tell me once, *"I have 20 years of experience!"* I thought, *"You have had 20, one year experiences."* Just because you have been around awhile does not guarantee anything.

Lucy Yeung, my good friend who I have adopted as my little sister would say when she described companies, *"Either you innovate, or you die!"* Which is so true! When you think about the public sector in particular, companies are at war! Either you come out with new and better products and or services, or you lose market share. Failure to innovate is the ultimate doom for a company. The same concept applies to individuals too. Failure to develop leads to a stalled and ultimately lackluster career.

I had to remind myself of this several years ago. For some reason I was fighting the urge to adapt to a smart phone. I was Blackberry Man! At the time, most people had smart phones. Well, when I joined the craze or the rest of the world, I had an iPhone 4S. Absolutely loved the phone! Fast forward several years later, and a little kid said, "Mister, why is your phone so small?" Of course that cracked everyone up that heard the question. Yeah, why is my phone so small. Well it was because I got so comfortable with my iPhone 4S, technology had passed me by. Heck, the new apps did not work, and I had to go to Amazon to by new cords because the stores quit carrying them.

Then I reminded myself of 23 year old Dan (myself) and what I wrote to myself. *Dissatisfaction is the base for progress, once you become satisfied, you become obsolete.* Well I had become complacent and was using outdated technology. The world was passing me by. The next day I ordered my iPhone X.

You can't hold on to the past if you want to move forward. The same with developing your talent, we should always look for the new way of doing things. Experience will always play a critical role in shaping your current career success, but embracing new adventures will push you to new career satisfaction and help you fulfill your true potential.

There will be times you will have to bend your job until it breaks. Reshape the role to get what you need out of it from a development perspective. You can do this by taking on other projects, tasks, or assignments to cover the development gap you are missing. It is extremely important to keep focusing on your development and not to fall into the complacency trap because it can easily happen to anyone.

Some of the best talented people I have worked for, worked with, and have worked for me have a common theme regarding their development, and that is they kept pursuing greatness in their field of work. Given the ever-changing fast pace of today's workplace you have to stay current on new methodologies, technologies, and strategies. To stay in the current mode, means to get passed on for promotions because you are not ready enough. To hold on to the present means to get left behind because of outdated thinking. Remember, people that own their development have a vision of where they are going and they keep moving even if they experience setbacks. There will always be something that could potentially derail your long term plan, but you must stay the course. Don't let a temporary setback define your career legacy.

About a year ago, during one of my trips home to Simpsonville, South Carolina to visit my parents I noticed my father had redecorated the living room. Gone were the many, and I mean many awards he had amassed over his illustrious military and corporate careers, and other pictures were on the wall. The same family pictures were there and a few new ones. Then it dawned on me how successful of a career my dad had both in the military and in the private work sectors.

So I tried to piece his career together from memory one night as I was sitting on the couch. My dad, Joseph Cohen Sr. is a great chef! But if you rewind his career, it started at a little hamburger joint in Greenwood, South Carolina. My dad went to work really early in life, and his first real job was cooking hamburgers. From the stories I've been told, my dad needed a real job if he planned on marring my mom (Margaret), so my dad joined the army. It was during his time in the army he became a mess Sergeant or what is known in the military as a cook. My dad simply loved to cook as he has a passion for cooking.

My dad would compete in cooking competitions and he would bring back blue ribbons, trophies, and a bunch of Polaroid pictures of the things he had prepared. Who knew you could make an orchestra out of shrimp and lobsters with mini instruments! Giant six foot ice carvings of swans, horns of plenty, and sea shells. The horn of plenty was stuffed with fruit and had colored lights in the background that gave an awesome reflection. The sea shells were stuffed with prawns and were always a big hit. My dad clearly finished his first career on top of his culinary game. But he was not finished.

After spending 21 years in the army, my dad retired. Barely in his forties, my dad started his 2nd and 3rd careers. The second being a manager and or director of various organizations as their top chef. But it was the 3rd career that was interesting to me, because it was *Marg and Joe's Catering*. Yes, dad started his catering business. I was put to work on the weekends we had business to do. One of my jobs was to draw the outline of whatever my dad was going to carve out of ice. Chain saw, ice, lots of noise and wham! A swan appears. My dad made it look so EASY. But what I did not know at the time, being a chef and a creative one at that was my talent. Plus he loved doing it. My dad was a perfectionist too! Everything had to be right all the way down to the little things like folding a napkin.

Each of my sister's weddings had featured my dad's culinary skills. People begin to ask my parents to cater their weddings and parties. We were a busy family. I recall during this time my dad going to Cornell University to take some courses, and he began teaching night classes at the local technical school too. What I realized is that my dad never stopped working on his career. He kept getting better and better. When dignitaries came to the region, my dad is who they called to do the meal. When you are great at what you do, others will seek you out. And my dad turned down a lot of work too, because if you were not willing to invest to get the best, then he was not going to tarnish his brand and settle for less.

What I did not appreciate at the time as a teenager was that working hard at whatever you do was important. Yes, I know I had to work hard, and I did at my early in career jobs. But I did not know WHY work hard. Good employees work hard. But work hard at what! Years later I learned that you have to put in effective effort. You work hard but on the right stuff. Work hard on the stuff that makes you better. Work on your talent(s) and improve the knowledge, skills and abilities that make you uniquely you. What got you to where you are today are your talents, and what will propel you into the future are your talents.

Chapter Nine
End Game

Every day is one day closer to completing your career journey. How we choose what that day looks like is up to the career decisions we make on a daily basis. Yes daily. It's the daily development activities that prepare you to be ready enough to compete for new career opportunities. When you put in effective effort you get better at what you do, and when you get better you get noticed. Great players get to have playing time and greatness is what gets noticed.

A sponsor selects and advocates for people that have performed well and have a great brand. When the time comes for you and a sponsor selects you, just know you are ready enough because leaders would not be tapping you if you were not ready. Just make sure whatever you are being asked to do supports your development plan. What do you plan to get out of doing the role and how does it help you move your career forward.

There is always time to do what you are passionate about. So never feel like time has expired on your career. Make a new path and literally do what you love to do. Some of the most successful people in history have started their careers later in life. Peter Roget was 73 when he invented the thesaurus. Julia Child began cooking in her late 30's. Van Gogh didn't start painting until his late 20's. Harlan David

Sanders, Colonel Sanders started Kentucky Fried Chicken at 65. Maybe one of the benefits of having success later in life is that you have a lot of experience to draw upon when you take on a new opportunity.

Most likely you have heard of the saying, begin with the end in mind. Picture where you will be at the end of your career journey. How many leaders will you have developed? What will you improve or change in your line of work? Or what does success look like for you? No matter how small or large it's how you define success. Only you can determine what success is for you and everyone else has their opinion.

As for me, I help people, teams and organizations reach their maximum potential, and I achieve this through executing world class HR practices. Each day when I come to work, this is my mission. It's also my brand and at the end of my career, others will judge if I met up to my expectations. You see when I meet with individuals I ask myself, did I meet their needs? When I look at how my teams are performing or not? I ask, am I doing my best to make sure they are reaching their maximum potential as a team. And at the end of each business quarter and year-end reviews, I ask did my organizations improve? You see, I need to keep a measurement of how I am living up to my end game. There will come a time, when you leave the organization and your legacy is set. It's then I hope you can look back on a career that is one of satisfaction and reward.